MW00612306

PRAISE

This is the first anthology I have seen that collects contemporary haiku from every continent, every nook and cranny of our planet. Pairing Japanese masters of the past with people writing haiku right now, *The Awakened One* is full of little zap insights. You feel that thrill, that quick wake-up to the ordinary, when the junky human stuff drops away and our world feels moist, tender, and real. Why has haiku been equated for so long with Buddhist insight? Pull this packet, compiled by Adjei Agyei-Baah and Gabriel Rosenstock, from your hip pocket. You might find your original self peeking from these little poems.

ANDREW SCHELLING
editor *The Wisdom Anthology of North American Buddhist Poetry*

THE AWAKENED ONE

THE AWAKENED ONE

Buddha-Themed Haiku from Around the World

Adjei Agyei-Baah
Gabriel Rosenstock

awaken ~ be still ~ drop the ego ~ awaken

POETRY CHAIKHANA

POETRY CHAIKHANA
www.poetry-chaikhana.com

ISBN: 978-0-9854679-9-9

Introduction

May this pocket anthology of haiku be of real benefit to all who dip into it!

A haiku is an awakening and the Buddha is The Awakened One who wishes all of us to come to an awakening, sooner or later. Yes, a true haiku is a true awakening. It is an awakening to universal insights experienced by people of all beliefs and none: 'The mind can go in a thousand directions, but on this beautiful path, I walk in peace. With each step, the wind blows. With each step, a flower blooms.' This is the Buddhist mind, the open, universal mind, the awakened mind, the joyous mind (even in hard times), the haiku mind as expressed beautifully above by Thich Nhat Hanh.

Haiku can become 'this beautiful path' which the Vietnamese monk describes for us so tenderly; and it can become a daily practice, too: reading haiku, writing haiku, illustrating haiku, translating haiku, experiencing its glow.

This anthology contrasts haiku by major and minor Japanese *haijin* (haiku masters) with contemporary practitioners. We could have filled it a thousand times over. But that would have contradicted the spirit of haiku which is a paring back to the essential, to the unclothed, mysterious trembling Void behind and beyond all phenomena and the Spirit that moves all things. May haiku flourish and flower in all lands and in all languages!

–The Editors

To readers

All versions of Japanese classics are by the Editors and may be reproduced freely. Kindly acknowledge the anthology.

enlightenment
is straightly attained by freedom
from separate selfhood

—BUDDHA

heavenly mystery . . .
autumn leaves
descend on a stone buddha

Imaizumi Sogetsu-ni (1750–1804)

sudden wind
the garden buddha's head crowned
with cherry blossoms

rafale de vent
le bouddha du jardin couronne
de fleurs de cerisier

Olivier Schopfer
(Switzerland)

on the old door . . .
the flickering shadow
of a swallow

Shōha (1727–1771)

lamp light
Buddha's features
flicker

Anne Curran
(New Zealand)

wild geese descend
cry upon cry . . .
frosty night

Morikawa Kyoroku (1656–1715)

twilight—
a part of me too
with the honking geese

Jill Lange
(USA)

many solemn nights
blond moon, we stand and marvel . . .
sleeping our noons away

Matsunaga Teitoku (1571–1654)

hilltop buddha
moonlight in the emptiness
of his cupped hand

Katherine Raine
(New Zealand)

the mind grows still . . .
deep in the forest
drip! drip! drip!

Hosha (1885–1954)

emptying his thoughts
into the rising sun . . .
hilltop monk

*bepɔso ɔhoteni
yi n'adwendwen nyinaa
de gu owia mu*

**Adjei Agyei-Baah
(Ghana)**

beginning of spring
the first silent step
of the stork

Shōha (1727–1771)

Christmas bells—
self-realizing
the hard way

Luca Cenisi
(Italy)

though you grow cold,
don't draw close to the fire,
Snow-Buddha

Yamazaki Sōkan (1458–1546)

little Buddha
in the bottom drawer—
left behind

Jerome Gagnon
(USA)

O the dragonfly!
he has dressed himself in the
color of autumn

Hori Bakusui (1718–1783)

imitating the buddha
my smile too
painted on

*Mike Rehling
(USA)*

the spring sun
shows its power
between snowfalls

Shigeyori (1602–1680)

snow falls
an old monk
sets aside his beads

Robert Witmer
(Japan)

hearing the truth
he becomes a lake . . .
pure, tranquil, deep

—BUDDHA

sparrows flying
from scarecrow
to scarecrow

Sazanami (1870–1933)

last frost
a sparrow builds with
scarecrow's innards

Randall Herman
(USA)

sleeping alone
too sad it is!
voice of the male mosquito

Nun Chigetsu (1634–1718)

lazy afternoon
unpunished mosquito
on my foot

leniwe popołudnie
bezkarny komar
na mojej stopie

Wiesław Karliński
(Poland)

the gates alone remain
of some great Buddhist temple
on this withered plain

Masaoka Shiki (1867–1902)

the golden temple
on the wooded hillside
enveloped in cloud

David Burleigh
(Ireland/Japan)

14

crickets cry no more . . .
now one can hear
dewdrops falling

Rogetsu (1873–1928)

the stone Buddha
as if it does not exist
autumn fog

ere Buddha kan
bi eni pe ko si'mbe
oye erun

Anthony Itopa Obaro
(Nigeria)

its fleeting light vanishing
in the palm of my hand . . .
firefly

Kyorai Mukai (1651–1704)

some must wait . . .
water lilies receiving
morning light

cuid díobh ag fanacht . . .
súnn duilleoga báite
grian na maidine

Gabriel Rosenstock
(Ireland)

in a cloudy well
this one moon . . .
let us all adore it

Tagami Kikusha-ni (1753–1826)

cherry blossoms
the morning moon mingles
with the petals

trešnja u cvatu
stopljen s laticama
jutarnji mjesec

Tomislav Maretić
(Croatia)

blossoms fallen—
people's hearts
becoming quiet

Koyu-Ni (18th c.)

after mother's death
I am finding true happiness
in cherry blossoms

nakon majčine smrti
pronalazim pravu sreću
u cvjetovima trešnje

Goran Gatalica
(Croatia)

raven, did you just call my name
from shadowland?
. . . frosty morning

Shukabo (1717–1775)

midday sunshine
a trail of ants hurries in and out
of the dead crow's eye

Bill Wolak
(USA)

desolate moor . . .
I bow before a stone Buddha
illumined by lightning

Kakei (1648–1716)

living with it
in light and in shadow
the garden Buddha

Sylvia Forges-Ryan
(USA)

sad stories
whispered to the jellyfish
by the sea slug

Shōha (1727–1771)

sunrise
a caterpillar on the path
to the stone Buddha

Nikolay Grankin
(Russia)

ebb tide
a crab wary
of a footprint

Miki Rofu (1889–1964)

go slowly ferryman
so I can observe once more
the other bank

*polako lađaru
da još jednom vidim
drugu obalu*

**Nikola Đuretić
(Croatia)**

beyond this shore
the farther shore . . .
beyond the beyond

—BUDDHA

skylark in the heavens . . .
what do you think
of the boundless sky

Chiyo-ni (1703–1775)

mother's day . . .
looking for her star
in the sky

ден на майката . . .
търся звездата ѝ
в необятното небе

Tsanka Shishkova
(Bulgaria)

socks out to dry
in frosty sun—
shivers!

Utsuji (1881–1920)

last leaf on rowan tree
the wind won't
leave it alone

Martin Vaughan
(Ireland)

when my eyes fall out
of their sockets—
I wish to see the lotus!

Yamaoka Tesshū (1836–1888)

lotus viewing . . .
the flowering
within

Kala Ramesh
(India)

falling from my heart
the snows
of Shinano

Kobayashi Issa (1763–1828)

Shinobazu Pond—
even these withered lotuses
can lift my heart

Maeve O'Sullivan
(Ireland)

becoming a cow
would be fine—morning naps
and the evening cool

Kagami Shikō (1665–1731)

afternoon nap—
the long body
of Buddha

*Jim Kacian
(USA)*

night in autumn—
giving to the cat
what was given me by a dog

Santōka Taneda (1882–1940)

begging bowl
a plum tree contributes
with a petal

Zelyko Funda
(Croatia)

taking me along
my shadow comes home
from moon-viewing

Yamaguchi Sodō (1642–1716)

spare moment
I dust the cobwebs
from Buddha

Tim Gardiner
(United Kingdom)

ashes, my burnt hut
but wonderful the cherry
blooming on my hill

Tachibana Hokushi (1665–1718)

moth dust
on my thumb . . .
namu amida butsu

Dr. Randy Brooks
(USA)

end of the old year . . .
first thing to clean up—
yourself!

Butsugai Fusen (1795–1867)

four winds come
four winds go
the Self remains unchanged

άνεμοι τέσσερις
έρχονται και παρέρχονται
αμετάβλητος μένει ο Εαυτός

Kon Markogiannis
(Greece)

again and again
stitching the rows of barley
a butterfly

Sora (1649–1710)

new buddha
a butterfly perching
and unperching

*buddha ọhụrụ
na nru ucha na-egbu egbu
ma adighi-aghasa*

**Emmanuel Jessie Kalusian
(Nigeria)**

the traveler who hesitates

just creates dust

on the road

—BUDDHA

summer morning . . .
a child in deep poverty
drags a head of cabbage

Ippekiro Nakatsuka (1887–1946)

refugee camp . . .
the cricket chirps
in the broken vessel

کیمپ†گزین†پناہ
چھچھاہٹ†جھینگرکی
میں†مٹکے†ہوئے†ٹوٹے

Hifsa Ashraf
(Pakistan)

such a still water
even the dragonfly
splashes it with the tail
Tan Taigi (1709–1771)

shaking shuffling
Roshi's last koan—
Parkinson's
　(Keido Fukushima Roshi, 1933–2011)

Robert MacLean
(Canada)

how beautifully
the cow has slimmed down
in the summer fields

Nozawa Bonchō (1640–1714)

h u n g e r
he fills it with the lord's
holy name

Christina Chin
(Malaysia)

all night long
I listen to the autumn wind . . .
a mountain retreat

Sora (1649–1710)

shadows lengthen
the koel's call
unanswered

Marilyn Humbert
(Australia)

how warm—
the shadows of withered trees
stretching out their arms

Nakamura Tei-jo (1900–1988)

sunset glow
offshore island already
in shadow

Ivan Randall
(Australia)

sunlight . . .
passing through a butterfly
asleep

Takakuwa Rankō (1726–1798)

on the memorial bench
a butterfly
opens its wings

no assento memorial
uma borboleta
abre as suas asas

Corine Timmer
(Portugal)

Corine Timmer & Esperança Dickman (tr)

a traveling monk
vanishes in mist . . .
a distant bell

Meisetsu (1847–1926)

shinrin-yoku
the walk to *nibana*
has no end

Elancharan Gunasekaran
(Singapore)

the stars have already
opened
their autumn eyes

Ozaki Kōyō (1867–1903)

shooting stars—
picking the beads
of my rosary

jíjá ìràwò —
mò n ṣa ìlèkè
tèsùbá mi

Taofeek Ayeyemi
(Nigeria)

God's bounty—
this path across
a withered moor

Kawahigashi Hekigodo (1873–1937)

sun-bright zendo
the swirling silence
of dust motes

*Christopher Herold
(USA)*

a cricket chirps—
now my life
is clear

Hakuu (1911–1936)

Amithaba
a cricket chirps
in the rain

Tom Bierovic
(USA)

three things cannot be long
hidden: the sun, the moon
and the truth

—BUDDHA

midnight—no waves, no wind
empty boat
flooded with moonlight

Dōgen (1200–1253)

tadpoles—
the stars trembling

mormoloci—
stelele tremurâ

Mirela Brăilean
(Romania)

over the violets
a small breeze
passes by

Ontei Shinohara (1872–1926)

tea ceremony
gently held cups
of Buddha's tears

Ron C. Moss
(Australia)

heat in waves—
in the stones
angry reverberations

Katō Kyōtai (1732–1792)

this beach of pebbles
after the wave
my life rearranged

Gregory Piko
(Australia)

dearly, dearly
embracing the sun—
the fallen garden leaves

Ritō (1681–1755)

sweeping dead leaves
shrunken skin
of my feet

သစ်ရွက်ခြောက်များလွဲကျင်းရာ

တွန့်ရှုအရေဟာ

အိုင့်ခြေထောက်သာ

Su Wai Hlaing
(Burma/Australia)

51

garden gate
slamming and thwacking—
autumn wind

Fukuda Haritsu (1865–1944)

zen garden
the wind wanders
around Buddha

jardim zen
o vento vagueia
ao redor de Buda

Rosa Clement
(Brazil)

the faces of dolls
how aged I've become . . .
the way it is

Nun Seifu (1731–1814)

transience . . .
petal by petal
we let go

Debbie Strange
(Canada)

my eyes
having observed everything
return to the white chrysanthemums

Kosugi Isshō (1653–1688)

Ryoanji
eye to eye with a stone—
we meditate

Ryoanji
Ochi în ochi cu o piatră—
Meditām

Marius Chelaru
(Romania)

I pursue the light
of the swift-footed lantern
through the chilly night

Takahama Kyoshi (1874–1959)

show me
your simple face
not your original face

Bruce England
(USA)

how easily it burns
how easily it goes out . . .
firefly

Chine-Jo (1660–1688)

firefly
forget
your short life

krijesnico
zaboravi
svoj kratki život

Drago Štambuk
(Croatia)

is it a foster child clinging to me?
this cricket
in my bedding

Ichikawa Dunjūrō (1660–1704)

sumo wrestlers
bow to Buddha
before the bout

Ljubomir Radovančević
(Croatia)

understand! the body is merely

the foam of a wave . . .

shadow of a shadow

—BUDDHA

summer moon!
is there a shortcut
through the clouds?

Den Sutejo (1634–1698)

my ancestors—
olive oil and wine pouring
through the same funnel

Svoje pretke
ulje i vino lijevam
istim lijevkom

Dragan Vucetic
(Croatia)

dragonflies
quiet their mad darting
crescent moon

Takarai Kikaku (1661–1707)

counting mala beads . . .
the silence of who I am

*Risë E. Daniels
(USA)*

on blades of grass
frolic and roll—
pearls of dew

Hattori Ransetsu (1654–1707)

spring morning
a sanitation worker
purifies Buddha

వసంతపు తెల్లవారు

ఓ పారిశుద్ధ్యపనివాడు

బుద్ధుడి మలినాన్ని తుడుస్తున్నాడు

Srinivasa Rao Sambangi
(India)

the scarecrow does not
uncover
even to His Imperial Majesty

Hōjō Dansui (1662–1711)

ancient tree
no fear of death
in its leaves

Anna Maris
(Sweden)

a lightning bolt
splits in two and strikes
the mountaintop

Naitō Jōsō (1662–1704)

clouds
where there is no mountain
a mountain

Margaret Beverland
(New Zealand)

autumn cemetery . . .
two or three fireflies
gadding about

Gensho (n.d.)

stone statue of Buddha . . .
two butterflies play
hide and seek

野仏とかくれんぼする蝶二匹

Ikuyo Yoshimura
(Japan)

things become clear:
the morning awakens
to the cuckoo's call

Ryōta Oshima (1718–1787)

hiking through birdsong
the track neither before
nor after

Mark Miller
(Australia)

first autumn morning:
the mirror I stare into
reflects father's face

Murakami Kijo (1865–1938)

morning cleansing
the last incense spirals a cloud
of clear thought

ಬೆಳಗಿನ ಶುದ್ಧೀಕರಣ

ಕೊನೆಯ ಧೂಪದ್ರವ್ಯದಿಂದ್ ಮೀಡವಾಗಿ

ಉದ್ಭವಿಸಿದ್ ಸ್ಪಷ್ಟ ಚಿಂತನೆಗಳು

Rashmi VeSa
(Bengaluru, India)

summer shower . . .
the worn-out horse
comes back to life

Takai Kitō (1741–1789)

walking in the park
with the rain

*разхождам се в парка
с дъжд*

**Nadejda Kostadinova
(Bulgaria)**

feeling lonely
he beats the gong again . . .
cabin guard

Sekitei Hara (1889–1951)

abandoned monastery
a tourist guide
in orange robe

Mohammad Azim Khan
(Pakistan)

like the peaks

of the Himalayas . . .

good men shine from afar

—BUDDHA

candle offered
to a dark Buddha . . .
scent of chrysanthemums

Sugita Hisajo (1890–1946)

the Medicine Buddha . . .
his lapis-lazuli-blue body

Ursula Maierl
(Austria/Australia)

no strength left—
I wrap my arms around my knees
in winter solitude

Shida Yaba (1662–1740)

above, the old stone
urges the faltering youth:
"to strive is enough"

Stanley H. Barkan
(USA)

calmly they fall
when their time comes—
poppy flowers

Ochi Etsujin (1656–1739)

dandelions . . .
die and are reborn
everywhere

*soffione
muoiono e rinascono
ovunque*

**Carmela Marino Sacco
(Rome)**

tumbling down
among the poppies . . .
grappling sparrows

Shirao (1738–1791)

macaque chatter
a star lily blooms
in silence

makimaki kōrerorero
puāwaitia te rengarenga whetū
noho puku

Jahan Tyson
(New Zealand/Australia)

visiting family graves
the old dog walks
ahead

Kobayashi Issa (1763–1827)

cold morning—
a leash leads me
into fog

शीत सुबह—
धुंद मे ले जा रही
एक चेन

Arvinder Kaur
(Chandigarh, India)

time oozes from my pores
drinking tea,
I tasted the seven seas

Shinkichi Takahashi (1901–1987)

tea ceremony
a plum blossom drifts
into my cup

Lucy Whitehead
(United Kingdom)

wake butterfly—
it's late, we have miles
to go together

Matsuo Basho (1644–1694)

cold to the touch
a heavy chain lock
on the temple's door

Duro Jaiye
(Japan)

on the temple bell
resting and dreaming . . .
a butterfly

Yosa Buson (1716–1784)

on the wooden steps
deepening the temple's silence
three cats

*sur les marches en bois
intensifiant le silence du temple
trois chats*

**Gilles Fabre
(France/Ireland)**

the sound
of one splash—
all the frogs jump in

Wakyu (d. 1759)

solid faith
devotees pray to
a headless buddha

iman yang padu
penganut memuja
buddha terpenggal

John Tiong Chinghoo
(Malaysia)

Adrina Omar (tr)

all are asleep
nothing comes between us . . .
the moon and I

Enomoto Seifu-jo (1731–1814)

moonlit night—
little statue of Buddha
among the bamboos

noite de lua—
estátua do pequeno Buda
entre os bambus . . .

Vanice Zimerman
(Brazil)

enjoy the mastery

of your hands and your feet . . .

your words and thoughts

—BUDDHA

I meditate
a mud snail begins
to walk

Ozaki Hōsai (1885–1926)

meditation
the breath
I am

Owen Bullock
(Australia)

at the sound of the sea
the sunflowers open
their black eyes

Yūji Kinoshita (1914–1965)

morning star—
the dark circles under
Siddhartha's eyes

*Clifford Rames
(USA)*

rolling up the blind . . .
I look out
at a changed world

Zen Master Chokei (1853–1932)

worldwide conflict
which leaf is more beautiful
in autumn?

Marisa Fazio
(Australia)

this autumn
I'll be looking at the moon
with no child on my knee

Uejima Onitsura (1661–1738)

working day eight hours—
how could he sit so long
Buddha?

osamsatni radni dan—
toliko sjedenja,
moj Buda!

Djurdja Vukelic Rozic
(Croatia)

sweetly arranged wreaths
on a coffin . . .
here comes a butterfly

Naito Meisetsu (1847–1926)

after rain—
a monarch butterfly
settles in his lap

മഴയ്ക്ക് ശേഷം-
ഒരു ശമോണോർക് ചിത്രലേഭം
അദ്ദെഹരിന്ദെ മടിയ്കിൽ കിടക്കുന്നു

Nisha Raviprasad
(India)

in my hermitage
all that I need . . .
wind in the pines

Ōtagaki Rengetsu (1791–1875)

old goat
climbing into a greater
solitude

Anatoly Kudryavitsky
(Ireland)

About the Editors

Adjei Agyei-Baah

Adjei Agyei-Baah is the co-founder of the Poetry Foundation Ghana, the Africa Haiku Network, and *The Mamba*, Africa's first international haiku journal. He writes from Ghana and is a leader in the growing haiku movement of Afriku in Africa.

africahaikunetwork.wordpress.com

Gabriel Rosenstock

Gabriel Rosenstock is a poet, haikuist, tankaist, novelist, playwright, short story writer, blogger and translator.

www.rosenstockandrosenstock.com

Made in the USA
Monee, IL
10 September 2021

76892171R00059